D0521478

Microsoft® Word 2016

Level **3**

Workbook

Rutkosky • Roggenkamp • Rutkosky

PARADIGM
EDUCATION SOLUTIONS

St. Paul

Senior Vice President	Linda Hein
Editor in Chief	Christine Hurney
Director of Production	Timothy W. Larson
Production Editor	Jen Weaverling
Cover and Text Designer	Valerie King
Copy Editors	Communicáto, Ltd.
Senior Design and Production Specialist	Jack Ross
Design and Production Specialist	PerfecType
Assistant Developmental Editors	Mamie Clark, Katie Werdick
Testers	Janet Blum, Fanshawe College; Traci Post
Instructional Support Writers	Janet Blum, Fanshawe College; Brienna McWade
Indexer	Terry Casey
Vice President Information Technology	Chuck Bratton
Digital Projects Manager	Tom Modl
Vice President Sales and Marketing	Scott Burns
Director of Marketing	Lara Weber McLellan

Trademarks: Microsoft is a trademark or registered trademark of Microsoft Corporation in the United States and/or other countries. Some of the product names and company names included in this book have been used for identification purposes only and may be trademarks or registered trade names of their respective manufacturers and sellers. The authors, editors, and publisher disclaim any affiliation, association, or connection with, or sponsorship or endorsement by, such owners.

We have made every effort to trace the ownership of all copyrighted material and to secure permission from copyright holders. In the event of any question arising as to the use of any material, we will be pleased to make the necessary corrections in future printings.

Cover Photo Credits: © Photomall/Dreamstime.com

Paradigm Publishing is independent from Microsoft Corporation, and not affiliated with Microsoft in any manner. While this publication may be used in assisting individuals to prepare for a Microsoft Office Specialist certification exam, Microsoft, its designated program administrator, and Paradigm Publishing do not warrant that use of this publication will ensure passing a Microsoft Office Specialist certification exam.

ISBN 978-0-76386-763-8 (digital)
ISBN 978-0-76387-161-1 (print)

© 2017 by Paradigm Publishing, Inc.
875 Montreal Way
St. Paul, MN 55102
Email: educate@emcp.com
Website: ParadigmCollege.com

24 23 22 21 20 19 18   6 7 8 9 10 11 12

Contents

Chapter 1 Apply Advanced Formatting   1

Chapter 2 Formatting with Styles   9

Chapter 3 Creating Forms   17

Chapter 4 Creating Forms with Legacy Tools   25

Chapter 5 Using Outline View and Creating
a Table of Authorities   33

Chapter 6 Sharing Documents and
Customizing Word Options   39

Performance Assessment   47

Apply Advanced Formatting

Study Tools

Study tools include a presentation and a list of chapter Quick Steps and Hint margin notes. Use these resources to help you further develop and review skills learned in this chapter.

Concepts Check

Check your understanding by identifying application tools used in this chapter. If you are a SNAP user, launch the Concepts Check from your Assignments page.

Recheck

Check your understanding by taking this quiz. If you are a SNAP user, launch the Recheck from your Assignments page.

Skills Exercise

Additional activities are available to SNAP users. If you are a SNAP user, access these activities from your Assignments page.

Skills Assessment

Applying Your Skills

Demonstrate your knowledge of features learned in this chapter by completing the following assessments.

Assessment

1

Data Files

Apply Character Spacing and OpenType Features

1. Open **PRDonations.docx** and then save it with the name **1-PRDonations**.
2. Select the quote text *"In every community there is work to be done. In every nation there are wounds to heal. In every heart there is the power to do it."* and then apply stylistic set 4. (Do this at the Font dialog box with the Advanced tab selected.)
3. Select the heading *Domestic Donations*, change the scale to 90%, and then change the spacing to Expanded. (Do this at the Font dialog box with the Advanced tab selected.)
4. Apply the same formatting in Step 3 to the heading *International Donations*.
5. Select the numbers in the *Domestic Donations* section. **Hint: To select only the numbers, position the mouse pointer at the beginning of $450,000, press and hold down the Alt key, use the mouse pointer to drag and select the four numbers in the second column, and then release the Alt key.** With the numbers selected, change the number spacing to Tabular spacing. (Do this at the Font dialog box with the Advanced tab selected.)
6. Select the numbers in the *International Donations* section and then change the number spacing to Tabular spacing.

7. Select the text *We are dedicated to working toward a more just and peaceful world.* and then insert a check mark in the *Use Contextual Alternates* check box at the Font dialog box with the Advanced tab selected.
8. Save, print, and then close **1-PRDonations.docx**.

Assessment 2

Data Files

Find and Replace Formatting and Use a Wildcard Character

1. Open **EmpGuide.docx** and then save it with the name **1-EmpGuide**.
2. Find text set in the +Headings font and replace the font with Candara.
3. Find text set in the +Body font and replace the font with Constantia.
4. Using a wildcard character, find all occurrences of *Ne?land?Davis* and replace them with *Newland-Davis*.
5. Save, print, and then close **1-EmpGuide.docx**.

Assessment 3

Data Files

Insert Fields in a Main Document

1. Open **BTVacsMD.docx** (at the message asking if you want to continue, click the Yes button) and then save it with the name **1-BTVacsMD**. (If a message displays asking if you want to continue, click the Yes button.)
2. Check to make sure the **1-BTDS.mdb** data source file is attached to the main document by clicking the Mailings tab and then clicking the Edit Recipient List button. (If the Edit Recipient List button is dimmed, the data source file is not attached.) At the Mail Merge Recipients dialog box, the file name **1-BTDS.mdb** should display in the *Data Source* list box. If the **1-BTDS.mdb** data source file is not attached, click the Select Recipients button, click the *Use an Existing List* option, navigate to the WL3C1 folder on your storage medium, and then double-click *1-BTDS.mdb*.
3. Press Ctrl + End to move the insertion point to the end of the document (below the file name **1-BTVacsMD.docx**).
4. Type Letter, press the spacebar, and then insert a Merge Record # field.
5. Move the insertion point immediately after the job title in the closing of the letter. Press the Enter key two times and then insert an If...Then...Else... field with the following specifications:
   a. At the Insert Word Field: IF dialog box, specify the *City* field in the *Field name* option box.
   b. Type Daly City in the *Compare to* text box.
   c. In the *Insert this text* text box, type the text shown below and then close the dialog box:

   P.S. A representative from Wildlife Eco-Tours will present information on upcoming tours at our Daly City branch office the first Saturday of next month. Come by and hear about exciting and adventurous eco-tours.

6. Merge the main document with the data source file.
7. Save the merged letters document and name it **1-BTVacsLtrs**.
8. Print and then close **1-BTVacsLtrs.docx**.
9. Save and then close **1-BTVacsMD.docx**.

Assessment 4

Data Files

Merge a Main Document with a Word Table Data Source File

1. Open **PRLtrMD.docx** and then save it with the name **1-PRLtrMD**.
2. Identify the Word table in the document named **PRClientTable.docx** as the data source file.
3. Insert the appropriate fields in the main document to insert the address block and the greeting line.

4. Move the insertion point to the end of the document and then insert a Merge Record # field one space after *Letter*.
5. Merge the main document with the data source file and then name the merged document **1-PRLetters**.
6. Print and then close **1-PRLetters.docx**.
7. Save and then close **1-PRLtrMD.docx**.

Assessment

5

Data Files

Record and Run Macros and Assign a Macro to the Quick Access Toolbar

1. Open **MacroText.docx** and then create a macro named XXXSubtitle (replacing *XXX* with your initials) with the following specifications:
   a. Position the insertion point at the beginning of the word *Heading* and then turn on the macro recorder.
   b. Press the F8 function key and then press the End key.
   c. Click the Center button and then click the Bold button.
   d. Change the font size to 14 points.
   e. Click the Shading button arrow and then click *Green, Accent 6, Lighter 40%* (last column, fourth row).
   f. Click the Borders button arrow and then click *Bottom Border* at the drop-down gallery.
   g. Turn off the macro recorder.
2. Create a macro named XXXDocFont (replacing *XXX* with your initials) that selects the entire document and then changes the font to Corbel. Assign the macro to the Quick Access Toolbar.
3. Close **MacroText.docx** without saving it.
4. Open **BusDocs.docx** and then save it with the name **1-BusDocs**.
5. Click the button on the Quick Access Toolbar that represents the XXXDocFont macro.
6. Run the XXXSubtitle macro for the four subtitles in the document: *Letter Formatting*, *Letter Styles*, *International Correspondence*, and *International Addresses*.
7. Keep the subtitle *International Correspondence* together with the paragraph that follows it. (Do this at the Paragraph dialog box with the Line and Page Breaks tab selected.)
8. Remove the XXXDocFont macro from the Quick Access Toolbar.
9. Save, print, and then close **1-BusDocs.docx**.

Assessment

6

Data Files

Record and Run a Macro with Fill-in Fields

1. At a blank document, record a macro named XXXNotSig (replacing *XXX* with your initials) that includes the information shown in Figure WB-1.1. Apply the No Spacing style and then set left tabs at the 0.5-inch mark, 1.5-inch mark, and 3-inch mark on the horizontal ruler. Include Fill-in fields in the macro at the three places the text is in parentheses. After inserting the *(county)* Fill-in field, press the Enter key and then end the macro recording.
2. Close the document without saving it.
3. Open **Agreement.docx** and then save it with the name **1-Agreement**.
4. Move the insertion point to the end of the document and then run the XXXNotSig macro and insert the following information when prompted:

   (name 1): LLOYD KOVICH
   (name 2): JOANNE MILNER
   (county): Ramsey County

5. Save, print, and then close **1-Agreement.docx**.

Figure WB-1.1 Assessment 6

```
STATE OF MINNESOTA   )
                     ) ss.
COUNTY OF RAMSEY     )

        I certify that I know or have satisfactory evidence that (name 1) and (name 2) are the persons
who appeared before me, and said persons acknowledge that they signed the foregoing Contract and
acknowledged it to be their free and voluntary act for the uses and purposes therein mentioned.



                                        _____
                                        NOTARY PUBLIC in and for the State of
                                        Minnesota residing in (county)
```

Assessment

7

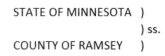

Create and Run a Macro with Fields

1. In this chapter, you learned how to create macros using Fill-in fields. You can also create macros using other fields at the Fields dialog box. At a blank document, record a macro named XXXEnd (replacing *XXX* with your initials) that completes the following steps:
   a. Change the line spacing to single (press Ctrl + 1).
   b. Insert the *FileName* field.
   c. Press the Enter key and then insert the *Date* field (with the default date format).
   d. Press the Enter key, type Number of Pages:, press the spacebar, and then insert the *NumPages* field (with the default format).
   e. Press the Enter key and then insert a Fill-in field that prompts the user to type his or her name.
2. Close the document without saving it.
3. Open **TechVisionaries.docx** and then save it with the name **1-TechVisionaries**.
4. Move the insertion point to the end of the document and then run the XXXEnd macro. At the prompt asking for your name, type your first and last names.
5. Save, print only the last page, and then close **1-TechVisionaries.docx**.

Visual Benchmark

Create Name Badge Labels for Conference Participants

1. Look at the information in the name badge labels in Figure WB-1.2. Using the information in the figure, create an Excel worksheet that will be used as a data source file that contains the information for each participant.
2. Save the Excel worksheet and name it **1-ConferenceDS**.
3. Print and then close **1-ConferenceDS.xlsx** and then close Excel.
4. At a blank document, click the Mailings tab, click the Start Mail Merge button, and then click *Labels* at the drop-down list.
5. At the Label Options dialog box, make sure the *Label vendors* option displays with *Avery US Letter*, click *45395 EcoFriendly Name Badges* in the list box (scroll up or down the list box to find this label), and then click OK.

6. Specify **1-ConferenceDS.xlsx** as the data source file. (Do this with the Select Recipients button.)
7. Insert the fields in the first label so the data will merge in the appropriate location and order in the label.
8. Update the labels.
9. Select the entire document and then apply formatting so the labels display with formatting similar to what is shown in Figure WB-1.2. (The font is Lucida Calligraphy.)
10. Merge the name badge labels.
11. Save the name badge label document and name it **1-NYNameTags**.
12. Print and then close **1-NYNameTags.docx**.
13. Save the name badge label main document and name it **1-NYBadgeMD**.
14. Print and then close **1-NYBadgeMD.docx**.

Figure WB-1.2 Visual Benchmark

Lawrence Vogel
Carter Center
New York
(212) 555-6427

Erin Bjorgen
Golden Sun Systems
New York
(212) 555-9005

Bryce Carmichael
Hartmann Construction
New York
(212) 555-7791

Ann Mansour
Interwest Industries
New York
(212) 555-8122

Teresa Guilding
Murrey Services
New York
(212) 555-2900

James Kagaki
Plaza Custom Designs
New York
(212) 555-1103

Frank Nichols
Summer Investments
New York
(212) 555-3945

Sarah Zimmerman
Valley Medical
New York
(212) 555-0095

Case Study

Part

1

Data Files

You are the assistant manager of Casa Verde, an Italian restaurant in downtown Seattle, Washington. One of your job responsibilities it to prepare the weekly specials menu. To expedite creating the menu and maintain consistency in formatting it, you decide to create a macro. At a blank document, type some text such as your name (that will be selected when creating the macro) and then create a macro with the following specifications:

- Name the macro XXXMenu (replacing *XXX* with your initials), assign it to the Quick Access Toolbar, and specify a button icon (using the Modify button at the Word Options dialog box). (You determine the macro description.)
- With the insertion point positioned at the beginning of the document, create a Fill-in field with the prompt *Type the current date.*
- Select the entire document and then apply the following formatting:
  ○ Display the Font dialog box with the Font tab selected, change the font to 16-point Gabriola, apply bold formatting, and change the font color to Green, Accent 6, Darker 50% (last column, last row in the *Theme Colors* section).
  ○ Display the Font dialog box with the Advanced tab selected, turn on kerning, apply stylistic set 2, and then close the Font dialog box.
  ○ Center the text.
  ○ Remove the spacing after paragraphs and apply 1.5 line spacing.
- End the recording of the macro.

Close the document without saving it. Open **CVMenu.docx** and then save it with the name **1-CVMenu**. Run the XXXMenu macro (from the Quick Access Toolbar) and type the date August 6, 2018 at the fill-in prompt. Save, print, and then close **1-CVMenu.docx**.

Part

2

Data Files

The chef at Casa Verde is now offering a chef's special on Fridays and Saturdays and you are responsible for formatting this special menu. Open **CVChefMenu01.docx** and then save it with the name **1-CVChefMenu01**. Run the XXXMenu macro (from the Quick Access Toolbar) and then type August 10, 2018 at the fill-in prompt. Save, print, and then close the menu. Open **CVChefMenu02.docx** and then save it with the name **1-CVChefMenu02.docx**. Run the XXXMenu macro and then type August 11, 2018 at the fill-in prompt. Save, print, and then close the menu. Delete the XXXMenu macro from the Macros dialog box and also remove the macro button from the Quick Access Toolbar.

Part

3

Data Files

To continue marketing Casa Verde to local hotels, you have put together an Excel worksheet with the names and addresses of hotels near the restaurant and Sea-Tac Airport and the name of the concierge or manager for each hotel. You want to send a letter each week to the concierge or manager of each hotel that includes the weekly specials menu. Open **CVLtrhd.docx** and then save it with the name **1-CVLtrsMD**. Identify the Excel worksheet **CVHotelsDS.xlsx** as the data source file. Type a letter using the date *August 3, 2018*. Insert the appropriate address block field and greeting line field. In the first paragraph of the letter, mention that the restaurant is offering weekly specials and that you think the patrons of the hotel will enjoy the restaurant's food and atmosphere. Mention that the weekly specials menu is enclosed with the letter. Use language that portrays the restaurant in a favorable manner and encourages the hotel concierge or manager to recommend the restaurant to hotel patrons. You may want to include an additional paragraph about the restaurant. For the last paragraph in the letter, insert an If...Then...Else... field that will insert the following paragraph in the letter if the hotel is *not* located in Seattle.

Casa Verde has a contract with Puget Sound Transport that offers a 20 percent discount for taxi service from hotels near the airport to the restaurant. When making a taxi reservation for hotel patrons to our restaurant, please contact Puget Sound Transport at 425-555-3499.

Type an appropriate complimentary close for the letter and include your reference initials and an enclosure notation (indicating that the weekly specials menu is enclosed with the letter). Merge the main document with the data source file and then save the merged letters as **1-CVHotelLetters**. Print and then close **1-CVHotelLetters.docx** and then save and close **1-CVLtrsMD.docx**.

Formatting with Styles

Study tools include a presentation and a list of chapter Quick Steps and Hint margin notes. Use these resources to help you further develop and review skills learned in this chapter.

Check your understanding by identifying application tools used in this chapter. If you are a SNAP user, launch the Concepts Check from your Assignments page.

Check your understanding by taking this quiz. If you are a SNAP user, launch the Recheck from your Assignments page.

Skills Exercise

Additional activities are available to SNAP users. If you are a SNAP user, access these activities from your Assignments page.

Skills Assessment

Assessment

1

Data Files

Create and Apply Styles to a Committee Report

1. Open **KMStyles.docx** and then save it with the name **2-KMStyles**.
2. Create a style based on the formatting of the *KodiakTitle* text and name it *KodiakTitle*. (Make sure you select the paragraph symbol with the text.)
3. Press Ctrl + End to move the insertion point to the end of the document and then create a new style named *KodiakQuote*. Apply the following formatting at the Create New Style from Formatting expanded dialog box:
   a. Change the left and right indents to 0.5 inch and the spacing after paragraphs to 12 points. ***Hint: Display these formatting options by clicking the Format button in the lower left corner of the dialog box and then clicking* Paragraph.**
   b. Click the Italic button.
   c. Change the font color to standard dark blue.
   d. Insert a blue single-line top border and a blue single-line bottom border. ***Hint: Display these formatting options by clicking the Format button and then clicking* Border.**
4. At the document, press the Up Arrow key and then create a style named *KodiakHeading* and apply the following formatting:
   a. Change the font to Copperplate Gothic Bold.
   b. Change the font color to standard blue.
5. Save the styles you created in a style set named with your three initials followed by *Kodiak*.
6. Save and then close **2-KMStyles.docx**.

7. Open **KMReport.docx** and then save it with the name **2-KMReport**.
8. Change to the style set named with your initials followed by *Kodiak*.
9. Apply the KodiakTitle style to the two titles in the document: *Audit Committee Report* and *Compensation Committee Report*.
10. Apply the KodiakHeading style to the four headings in the report: *Committee Responsibilities*, *Fees to Independent Auditor*, *Compensation Philosophy*, and *Competitive Compensation*.
11. Apply the KodiakQuote style to the second paragraph of text in the document (the paragraph that begins *Assist the company's board of directors*).
12. Edit the KodiakTitle style by changing the font color to standard dark blue and underlining the text.
13. Edit the KodiakHeading style by changing the font color to standard dark blue.
14. Turn on the display of the Styles task pane and then display all the styles in alphabetical order. ***Hint: Do this at the Style Pane Options dialog box.***
15. Select the bulleted text in the *Committee Responsibilities* section and then apply the Block Text style. With the text still selected, click the Font Color button on the Home tab and then click the *Dark Blue* color option in the *Standard Colors* section.
16. Select the bulleted text in the *Compensation Philosophy* section, apply the Block Text style, and then change the font color to standard dark blue.
17. Save the modified styles as a style set with the same name (your initials followed by *Kodiak*). (At the Save as a New Style Set dialog box, click your style set name in the Content pane and then click the Save button. At the message asking if you want to replace the existing file, click the Yes button.)
18. Save and then print **2-KMReport.docx**.
19. Select and then delete the contents of the document (except the header).
20. Save the document as a template (in the Custom Office Templates folder) and name it **XXX-KMStyles** (using your initials in place of the *XXX*).
21. Close the template.

Create and Apply Multilevel List and Table Styles

Assessment

2

Data Files

1. Open **KMListTable.docx**.
2. Click the Multilevel List button in the Paragraph group on the Home tab, click *Define New List Style*, and then create a style named *KMList*. Apply the following formatting at the Define New List Style dialog box:
   a. For the first level of the numbered list, change the font to Cambria, apply bold formatting, and change the font color to standard dark blue.
   b. For the second level, specify the snowflake symbol (❋) as the bullet, apply bold formatting, and change the font color to standard dark blue. ***Note: The snowflake symbol is character code 84 in the Wingdings font.***
3. At the document, select and then delete the contents of the document (except the header).
4. Save the document as a template (with the *.dotx* extension) with the name **XXX-KMListTable** (using your initials in place of the *XXX*).
5. Close the template.
6. Open a document based on **XXX-KMListTable.dotx**. ***Hint: Do this at the New backstage area.***
7. Insert **KMAgendas.docx** into the current document.
8. Change to the style set named with your initials followed by *Kodiak*.
9. Apply the KodiakTitle style to the title *Kodiak Annual Meeting*.

10. Apply the KodiakHeading style to the two headings in the document: *Finance Department Agenda* and *Research Department Agenda*.

11. Select the text below the *Finance Department Agenda* heading and then apply the KMList multilevel list style. **Hint: Do this with the Multilevel List button in the Paragraph group on the Home tab.**

12. Select the text below the *Research Department Agenda* heading and then apply the KMList multilevel list style.

13. Save the document with the name **2-KMAgendas**.

14. Print and then close **2-KMAgendas.docx**.

15. In Word, open the template **XXX-KMListTable.dotx** from the Custom Office Templates folder in the Documents folder on your local hard drive.

16. Create a table style at the Create New Style from Formatting dialog box with the following specifications:

   a. Type KMTable in the *Name* text box.

   b. At the expanded Create New Style from Formatting dialog box, change the *Style type* to *Table*.

   c. For the whole table, change the font to Cambria and the color to standard dark blue, click the Border button arrow and then click *All Borders*, and then, if necessary, change the border color to standard blue.

   d. For the header row, change the font size to 12 points; apply bold formatting; change the font color to White, Background 1; and apply the Blue, Accent 1, Darker 25% fill color (fifth column, fifth row in the *Theme Colors* section).

   e. For the odd banded rows, apply the Blue, Accent 1, Lighter 80% fill color (fifth column, second row in the *Theme Colors* section).

17. Save and then close **XXX-KMListTable.dotx**.

18. Press Ctrl + N to display a blank document and then delete the XXXKodiak style set (where your initials display in place of the *XXX*).

Organize Styles

1. With a blank document open, display the Organizer dialog box. **Hint: Click the Styles group task pane launcher, click the Manage Styles button, and then click the Import/Export button.**

2. At the Organizer dialog box, click the Close File button below the left list box and then click the Open File button. At the Open dialog box, click the *Documents* folder in the Navigation pane, double-click the *Custom Office Templates* folder in the Content pane, and then double-click **XXX-KMListTable.dotx**.

3. Click the Close File button below the right list box and then click the Open File button. At the Open dialog box, click the *Documents* folder in the Navigation pane, double-click the *Custom Office Templates* folder in the Content pane, and then double-click **XXX-KMStyles.dotx**.

4. Copy the KMList and KMTable styles from the left list box in the Organizer dialog box to the right list box and then close the dialog box. At the message that displays asking if you want to save the changes to XXX-KMStyles.dotx, click the Save button.

5. Open a document based on **XXX-KMStyles**. **Hint: Do this at the New backstage area.**

6. Insert **KMSales.docx** and then save the document with the name **2-KMSales**.

7. Apply the KodiakTitle style to the title *Quarterly Sales*.

8. Apply the KodiakHeading style to the four headings in the document.

9. Apply the KMTable style to the four tables in the document.
10. Save, print, and then close **2-KMSales.docx**.
11. Close the Styles task pane and then close the blank document without saving the changes.

Assessment

4

Modify a Predesigned Table Style

1. In this chapter, you learned how to create a table style and apply all the formatting to the style. You can also create a style based on an existing predesigned table style. At a blank document, insert a table with a couple of rows and columns and then determine how to modify an existing table style. After experimenting with modifying a table style, close the document without saving it.
2. Open **NSSTables.docx** and then save it with the name **2-NSSTables**.
3. Click in any cell in the top table and then click the Table Tools Design tab.
4. Modify the List Table 1 Light - Accent 1 table style (second column, first row in *List Tables* section) by changing the name to *NSSTable* and then apply the following formatting:
   a. For the whole table, change the font to Candara and change the cell alignment to Align Center. ***Hint: The alignment button is right of the Fill Color option.***
   b. For the whole table, change the table alignment to Center. ***Hint: Do this at the Table Properties dialog box with the Table tab selected. Display this dialog box by clicking the Format button and then clicking* Table Properties**.
   c. For the header row, change the fill color to Blue, Accent 1, Lighter 60% (fifth column, third row in the *Theme Colors* section).
   d. For the first column, change the alignment to Align Center Left and remove the bold formatting.
   e. For the odd banded rows, apply the Green, Accent 6, Lighter 80% fill color (last column, second row in the *Theme Colors* section).
   f. For the even banded rows, apply the Blue, Accent 1, Lighter 80% fill color (fifth column, second row in the *Theme Colors* section).
5. After modifying the table style, apply it to the four tables in the document. (The NSSTable style is in the *List Tables* section of the drop-down gallery.)
6. Save, print, and then close **2-NSSTables.docx**.

Visual Benchmark

Data Files

Create and Apply Styles

1. Open **ELSInvoice.docx** and then save it with the name **2-ELSInvoice**.
2. Format the title *Monthly Invoices* as shown in Figure WB-2.1. (The text in the document is formatted with the font Gills Sans MT font.)
3. Format the subtitle *August, 2018* as shown in the figure.
4. Create a style named *XXX-ELSTitle* with the formatting of the title text. (Insert your initials in place of the *XXX*.)
5. Create a style named *XXX-ELSSubtitle* with the formatting of the subtitle text. (Insert your initials in place of the *XXX*.)
6. Create a table style named *XXX-ELSTable* with the formatting shown in the table in Figure WB-2.1. (To center the table in the table style, click the Format button in the lower left corner of the Create New Style from Formatting dialog box and then click *Table Properties* at the drop-down list. At the Table Properties dialog box, click the *Center* option in the *Alignment* section.)

12   Word Level 3

Chapter 2 | Formatting with Styles

Monthly Invoices

August, 2018

Invoice #	Client #	Service	Date	Amount
1010	10-788	Lawn maintenance	06/04/2018	$60.00
1011	11-279	Moss control	06/04/2018	$50.00
1012	11-279	Seasonal pruning	06/05/2018	$80.00
1013	06-411	Lawn mowing	06/06/2018	$40.00
1014	04-523	Debris removal	06/07/2018	$30.00
1015	10-788	Lawn maintenance	06/11/2018	$60.00
1016	06-411	Lawn mowing	06/12/2018	$40.00
1017	02-988	Weed control	06/12/2018	$55.00
1018	04-325	Lawn maintenance	06/13/2018	$60.00
1019	10-788	Seasonal pruning	06/14/2018	$80.00
1020	10-788	Lawn maintenance	06/18/2018	$60.00
1021	06-411	Lawn mowing	06/19/2018	$40.00
1022	11-279	Tree trimming	06/20/2018	$95.00
1023	04-325	Debris removal	06/21/2018	$55.00
1024	38-539	Plant care	06/22/2018	$75.00
1025	10-788	Lawn maintenance	06/25/2018	$60.00
1026	20-549	Plant care	06/26/2018	$50.00
1027	11-279	Lawn mowing	06/27/2018	$40.00
1028	10-386	Moss control	06/28/2018	$50.00
1029	02-988	Fertilizing	06/29.2018	$45.00

5443 Camden Boulevard
Cascadia, CA 95346
(530) 555-5500

7. Apply the XXX-ELSTable style to the table in the document. (**Your document should appear similar to the one shown in Figure WB-2.1.**)
8. Save and then print **2-ELSInvoice.docx**.
9. Delete the text in the document (except the header and footer) and then save the document as a template with the name **XXX-ELS** in the Custom Office Templates folder.
10. Close **XXX-ELS.dotx**.
11. Open a document based on **XXX-ELS.dotx**. (Do this at the New backstage area.)
12. Insert **ELSTables.docx** into the open document. (Use the Object button in the Text group on the Insert tab.)
13. Apply the following styles:
    a. Apply the XXX-ELSTitle style to the title *June Weekly Invoices*.
    b. Apply the XXX-ELSSubtitle style to the four subtitles (*Week Ending June 8, Week Ending June 15*, and so on.)
    c. Apply the XXX-ELSTable style to the four tables.
14. Save the document and name it **2-ELSInvoices**.
15. Print and then close **2-ELSInvoices.docx**.

Case Study

Part 1

Data Files ▶

You have opened a new graphic design company named Triadic Designs and need to prepare styles for the company's correspondence. Open **TDLtrhd.docx** and then save it with the name **2-TDStyles**. Looking at the letterhead graphic and colors, create a title style, heading style, and quote style. You determine the formatting and names of the styles. Save the styles in a style set and name it *XXXTD* (using your initials in place of the *XXX*). Save and then close **2-TDStyles.docx**.

Part 2

You created a report on newsletter design for a Triadic Designs client and want to format it with the company's styles using the XXXTD style set. Open **TDReport.docx** and then save it with the name **2-TDReport**. Apply the XXXTD style set. Apply the title style you created in Part 1 to the titles *DESIGNING A NEWSLETTER* and *CREATING NEWSLETTER LAYOUT*. Apply the heading style you created to the headings *Applying Guidelines*, *Choosing Paper Size and Type*, *Choosing Paper Weight*, and *Creating Margins*. Apply the quote style you created to the first paragraph and last paragraph of text in the document. Save and then print **2-TDReport.docx**.

Part 3

To use the styles in the style set you created for Triadic Designs, you decide to save the document as a template. With **2-TDReport.docx** open, select all the report content and then delete it. Save **2-TDReport.docx** as a template in the Custom Office Templates folder and name it **XXX-TDStyles** (using your initials in place of the *XXX*). Open a new blank document and then use the Screenshot button in the Illustrations group on the Insert tab to make a screen clipping of the Home tab in **XXX-TDStyles.dotx**. (The styles gallery in the Styles group on the Home tab displays the styles you created for Triadic Designs.) Print the document containing the screen clipping and then close the document without saving it. Close **XXX-TDStyles.dotx**.

Part 4

Using the Internet, search for articles on graphic design techniques for letterheads. After reading several articles, open a document based on the template **XXX-TDStyles.dotx** and then create a document that describes at least three design techniques. Properly cite the website sources for the information you are using in the document. Use the styles you created for Triadic Designs to format the document. Save the completed document and name it **2-TDTechniques**. Print and then close **2-TDTechniques.docx**.

Part 5

At a blank document, write a memo to your instructor that describes the three styles you created for Triadic Designs. Include the name of each style and the formatting you applied to it. Save the completed memo document and name it **2-TDMemo**. Print and then close **2-TDMemo.docx**.

Creating Forms

Study Tools

Study tools include a presentation and a list of chapter Quick Steps and Hint margin notes. Use these resources to help you further develop and review skills learned in this chapter.

Concepts Check

Check your understanding by identifying application tools used in this chapter. If you are a SNAP user, launch the Concepts Check from your Assignments page.

Recheck

Check your understanding by taking this quiz. If you are a SNAP user, launch the Recheck from your Assignments page.

Skills Exercise

Additional activities are available to SNAP users. If you are a SNAP user, access these activities from your Assignments page.

Skills Assessment

Assessment

1

Data Files

Create and Fill in an Owner Information Form

1. Open **AACLtrhd.docx**, insert a continuous section break, and then change the left and right margins to 1.5 inches.
2. Create the form shown in Figure WB-3.1. Double-space between each line of text and insert a plain text content control one space after each colon, as indicated in the figure.
3. Select the document and then group the text and content controls.
4. Save the document as a template in the Custom Office Templates folder with the name **XXXOwnerForm** (using your initials in place of the *XXX*).
5. Close **XXXOwnerForm.dotx**.
6. Create a form document from the template **XXXOwnerForm.dotx** by completing the following steps:
   a. Click the File tab and then click the *New* option. At the New backstage area, click the *PERSONAL* option and then click the *XXXOwnerForm* thumbnail (where your initials display in place of the *XXX*).
   b. Enter the following information:

   > *Pet:* Lucy
   > *Owner's name:* Douglas and Cheryl Taylor
   > *Address:* 12215 North 32nd Street, Kearney, NE 68875
   > *Primary phone:* 308-555-3049
   > *Email address:* None
   > *Emergency contact:* Ellen Taylor
   > *Emergency phone:* 308-555-6871

7. Save the document with the name **3-TaylorInfo**.
8. Print and then close **3-TaylorInfo.docx**.

Figure WB-3.1 Assessment 1

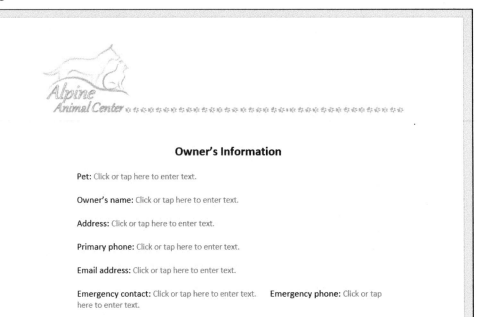

Owner's Information

Pet: Click or tap here to enter text.

Owner's name: Click or tap here to enter text.

Address: Click or tap here to enter text.

Primary phone: Click or tap here to enter text.

Email address: Click or tap here to enter text.

Emergency contact: Click or tap here to enter text.   Emergency phone: Click or tap here to enter text.

Assessment 2

Edit and Fill in the Owner Information Form

1. Open **XXXOwnerForm.dotx** (where your initials display in place of the *XXX*) from the Custom Office Templates folder. (Make sure you open the template and not a document based on the template.)
2. Display the form in design mode and then make the following edits:
   a. Change *Pet:* to *Pet's name:*.
   b. Position the insertion point to the right of the content control after *Primary phone:*, press the Tab key, type Secondary phone:, press the spacebar, and then insert a plain text content control.
3. Save and then close **XXXOwnerForm.dotx**.
4. Create a form document from the template **XXXOwnerForm.dotx** (do this at the New backstage area) and then enter the following information:

   Pet's name: Charlie
   Owner's name: Tamika Gray
   Address: 450 Sixth Avenue, Kearney, NE 68875
   Primary phone: 308-555-0394
   Secondary phone: 308-555-5538
   Email address: tgray@emcp.net
   Emergency contact: Roland Stevens
   Emergency phone: 308-555-1270

5. Save the document with the name **3-GrayInfo**.
6. Print and then close **3-GrayInfo.docx**.

Assessment 3

Data Files

Create and Fill in a Pet Boarding Form

1. Open **AACLtrhd.docx** and then save the document as a template in the Custom Office Templates folder with the name **XXXBoardingForm** (typing your initials in place of the *XXX*).

2. Press the Enter key and then create the form shown in Figure WB-3.2 with the following specifications:
   a. Create a table with four columns and five rows.
   b. Merge the first row of cells, change the row height to 0.5 inch, change the alignment to Align Center, and apply Green, Accent 6, Lighter 80% shading (last column, second row in the *Theme Colors* section). Change the font size to 16 points and then type the text in the cell.
   c. Select the four rows below the merged row, change the row height to 0.3 inch, and then change the alignment to Align Center Left.
   d. Type the text as indicated in the first and third columns.
   e. Insert plain text content controls in the second and fourth columns in the second and third rows.
   f. Insert date picker content controls in the second and fourth columns in the fourth row.
   g. Insert check boxes as indicated in the second and fourth columns in the fifth row.
3. Use options at the Restrict Editing task pane to protect the template. (You do not need to enter a password.)
4. Save and then close **XXXBoardingForm.dotx**.
5. Create a form document from the template **XXXBoardingForm** and insert the following data in the specified fields:

> *Owner:* Ralph Silva
> *Pet:* Jessie
> *Contact number:* 308-555-3028
> *Emergency number:* 308-555-8423
> *Arrival date:* (Insert the current date)
> *Pick-up date:* (Insert a date two days from the current date)
> *Bath:* (Click the *Yes* check box to insert a check mark)
> *Flea treatment:* (Click the *No* check box to insert a check mark)

6. Save the document with the name **3-JessieInfo**.
7. Print and then close **3-JessieInfo.docx**.

Figure WB-3.2 Assessment 3

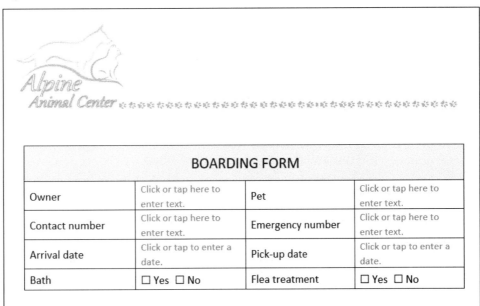

Create and Fill in a Pet Information Form

1. Open **AACPetInfo.docx** and then save the document as a template in the Custom Office Templates folder with the name **XXXPetForm** (typing your initials in place of the *XXX*).

2. Enter the text in cells as shown in Figure WB-3.3 and insert the following content controls:

    a. Insert a picture content control in the first cell in the table and then insert the image **AACLogo.jpg**.

    b. Insert a date picker content control for the date.

    c. Insert a plain text content control for the owner's name, pet's name, species, breed, coloring, gender, age, and neutered.

    d. Insert a drop-down list content control in the cell right of the cell containing *Overall health* and provide the title *Pet's health* and the following choices: *Poor, Fair, Good,* and *Excellent*.

    e. Insert check box form fields in the two rows of cells below the *Vaccinations* heading.

    f. Insert a drop-down list content control in the cell right of the cell containing *Preferred method of payment* and provide the title *Payment method* and the following choices: *Cash, Check,* and *Credit card*.

    g. Insert a combo box content control in the cell right of the cell containing *How did you hear about our center?* and provide the following choices: *Referral, Internet,* and *Friend*. (Do not include a title.)

3. Protect the template and only allow filling in the form. (You do not need to enter a password.)

4. Save and then close **XXXPetForm.dotx**.

5. Create a form document from the template **XXXPetForm.dotx** and insert the following data in the specified fields:

    Today's date: (Insert the current date)
    Owner's name: Jo Sarin
    Pet's name: Joey
    Species: Dog
    Breed: Beagle
    Coloring: Black, white, tan
    Gender: Male
    Age: 5
    Neutered: Yes
    Overall health: (Choose Good at the drop-down list)
    Rabies, DA22P, and *Parvo:* (Insert "X's" in these check boxes)
    Preferred method of payment: (Choose *Credit card* at the drop-down list)
    How did you hear about our center?: (Type Coworker—since that was not one of the options)

6. Save the document with the name **3-JoeyInfo**.

7. Print and then close **3-JoeyInfo.docx**.

Figure WB-3.3 Assessment 4

Today's date	Click or tap to enter a date.	Owner's name	Click or tap here to enter text.
Pet's name	Click or tap here to enter text.	Species	Click or tap here to enter text.
Breed	Click or tap here to enter text.	Coloring	Click or tap here to enter text.
Gender	Click or tap here to enter text.	Age	Click or tap here to enter text.
Neutered	Click or tap here to enter text.	Overall health	Choose an item.

Vaccinations			
☐ Rabies	☐ DA22P	☐ Parvo	☐ Bordetella
☐ Leukemia	☐ Calcivirus	☐ FVR	☐ FPV

Preferred method of payment	Choose an item.
How did you hear about our center?	Choose an item.

Assessment

5

Data Files

Create and Fill in a Client Information Form That Includes a Building Block Gallery Content Control

1. The Controls group on the Developer tab contains a Building Block Gallery Content Control button that inserts a content control for inserting building blocks in a form. Open **BGBuildingBlocks.docx** and create the following building blocks:
   a. Select the name *Barrington & Gates*, the line below, and the text *Rachel Rasmussen, Associate* and then save the selected text in a custom building block in the Quick Parts gallery named with your initials followed by *BGRR*.
   b. Select the name *Barrington & Gates*, the line below, and the text *Gerald Castello, Associate* and then save the selected text in a custom building block in the Quick Parts gallery named with your initials followed by *BGGC*.
   c. Close **BGBuildingBlocks.docx**.
2. Open **BGClientInfo.docx** and then save the document as a template in the Custom Office Templates folder with the name **XXXBGClientInfo.dotx** (typing your initials in place of the *XXX*).
3. Make the top cell active, click the Developer tab, and then click the Building Block Gallery Content Control button in the Controls group.
4. Select the entire table, turn on design mode, group the selected text and content controls, and then turn off design mode. (Because your template contains the building block gallery content control, you cannot protect it and allow only filling in the form. Doing this would keep you from being able to use the building block content control.)
5. Save and then close **XXXBGClientInfo.dotx**.

6. Create a form document from the template **XXXBGClientInfo.dotx** with the following specifications:
   a. Click the building block content control in the top cell, click the Explore Quick Parts tab that displays above the content control, and then click the *BGGC* building block that is preceded by your initials.
   b. Fill in each plain text content control by clicking the text *Click here to enter text* and then typing text of your choosing. Click the content control after *Payment Method:* and then click *Check* at the drop-down list.
7. Save the completed form document with the name **3-GCClient**.
8. Print and then close **3-GCClient.docx**.

Visual Benchmark

Create and Fill in an Application Form

1. Create the form shown in Figure WB-3.4 as a template and use the Tables feature to create the columns and rows. Apply border and shading formatting as shown in the figure. Set the company name in the Magneto font and set the remaining text in Candara.
2. Insert a picture content control and insert the image **SSAviation.png**. Insert date picker and plain text content controls in the appropriate cells. Insert drop-down list content controls for the two bottom rows in the table. Add the following options for the *Desired license:* drop-down list content control: *Private, Commercial, Instrument,* and *Certified Flight Instructor.* Add the following options for the *How did you hear about South Sound Aviation?* drop-down list content control: *Internet, Business card, Referral, Brochure,* and *Other.*
3. Protect the template and allow only filling in the form. Do not set a password.
4. Save the document as a template with the name **XXXSSAApplication** (using your initials in place of the *XXX*). Close the document.

Figure WB-3.4 Visual Benchmark

5. Create a form document from the template **XXXSSAApplication.dotx**. You determine the data to enter in each content control.
6. Save the document with the name **3-FlightApp**.
7. Print and then close **3-FlightApp.docx**.

Case Study

You just opened a bookstore named *Cornerstone Books* and want to create a letterhead and forms for it. First, create a letterhead that contains the store name *Cornerstone Books*; the address *1919 Roane Street, Charleston, WV*; the telephone number *681-555-1919*; and the email address *emcp.net/cornerstone*. Consider including an image with the letterhead. Search online for an image or use one of the images in the WL3C3 folder on your storage medium (CBImage01.png, CBImage02.png, CBImage03.png, or CBImage04.png). Create the letterhead in a header and/or a footer. Save the completed letterhead document with the name **3-CBLtrhd**.

Open **3-CBLtrhd.docx** and then save it as a template in the Custom Office Templates folder with the name **XXXCBMailingForm**. Create a mailing list request form for Cornerstone Books that includes the title *Mailing List Request* along with the following information (you determine the formatting of the information as well as what content controls to use in the form):

- First name
- Last name
- Address
- City
- State
- Zip code
- Telephone
- Birthday

Restrict the editing of the form and then save and close the form. Create a form document from the template **XXXCBMailingForm.dotx** and then fill in the form using data of your choosing. Save the completed document with the name **3-MailingRequest**. Print and then close **3-MailingRequest.docx**.

Open **3-CBLtrhd.docx** and then save it as a template in the Custom Office Templates folder with the name **XXXCBSurveyForm**. Create a survey form for Cornerstone Books in a table that includes the title *Reader Survey* along with the following information (you determine the formatting of the information as well as what content controls to use in the form):

- Today's date
- How often do you read? (Include the choices *Daily*, *Weekly*, and *Monthly*)
- Do you read for pleasure? (Include the choices *Yes*, *No*, and *Sometimes*)
- What do you prefer to read for pleasure? (Include the choices *Books*, *Magazines*, and *Newspapers*)
- Do you read for work? (Include the choices *Yes*, *No*, and *Sometimes*)
- What do you generally read for work? (Include the choices *Manuals*, *Journals*, and *Trade Magazines*)
- Where do you prefer to shop? (Include the choices *In store* and *Online*)

Restrict the editing of the form and then save and close it. Create a form document from the template **XXXCBSurveyForm.dotx** and then fill in the form using data of your choosing. Save the completed document with the name **3-Survey**. Print and then close **3-Survey.docx**.

Visit some online wholesale book sellers as well as other bookstores, such as Amazon.com. Search for a specific book that interests you and then look at the information that displays about it. Using some of the information at the websites as a guide, open **3-CBLtrhd.docx** and save it as a template in the Custom Office Templates folder with the name **XXXCBOrderForm**. Create a book order form for Cornerstone Books for purchasing books from a book distributor. Include the information needed to identify the book or books being ordered. Restrict editing of the form and then save and close it. Create a form document from the template **XXXCBOrderForm.dotx** and then fill in the form using data of your choosing. Save the completed document with the name **3-BookOrder**. Print and then close **3-BookOrder.docx**.

Creating Forms with Legacy Tools

Study Tools

Study tools include a presentation and a list of chapter Quick Steps and Hint margin notes. Use these resources to help you further develop and review skills learned in this chapter.

Concepts Check

Check your understanding by identifying application tools used in this chapter. If you are a SNAP user, launch the Concepts Check from your Assignments page.

Recheck

Check your understanding by taking this quiz. If you are a SNAP user, launch the Recheck from your Assignments page.

Skills Exercise

Additional activities are available to SNAP users. If you are a SNAP user, access these activities from your Assignments page.

Skills Assessment

Assessment

1

Data Files

Create and Fill in an Application Form

1. Open **ERCFundApp.docx** and then save the document as a template with the name **4-ERCFundForm** in the WL3C4 folder on your storage medium.
2. Enter the data in the appropriate cells and insert text and check box form fields in the template form, as shown in Figure WB-4.1.
3. Protect the template to allow only filling in the form. (You determine the password.)
4. Save and then close **4-ERCFundForm.dotx**.
5. Use File Explorer to create a form document from the template **4-ERCFundForm.dotx** and then insert the following data in the specified fields:

> *Project Title:* Quality Improvement Project
> *Date:* (Insert current date)
> *Targeted Department:* Pediatrics
> *Department Manager:* Angela Gilmore
> *Required Funds:* $50,000
> *Matching Funds:* $25,000
> *Beginning Date:* 07/01/2018
> *Completion Date:* 06/30/2019
> *Insert an X in each check box* except *Cost reduction.*
> *Applicant Name:* Maria Alvarez
> *Employee Number:* 321-4890
> *Department:* Pediatrics
> *Extension:* 4539

6. Save the document with the name **4-ERCFundApp**.
7. Print and then close **4-ERCFundApp.docx**.

Figure WB-4.1 Assessment 1

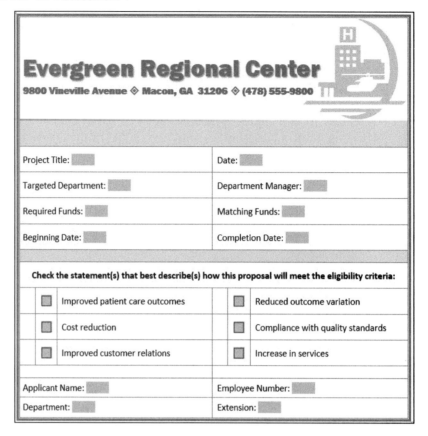

Assessment 2

Create and Fill in a Patient Update Form

1. Open **WCDSForm.docx** and then save the document as a template with the name **4-WCDSForm** in the WL3C4 folder on your storage medium.
2. Enter the data in the appropriate cells and insert form fields in the form as shown in Figure WB-4.2 with the following specifications:
   a. Insert a text form field for *Patient Number:* that specifies a maximum length of four characters.
   b. Insert a text form field for *State:* that specifies a maximum length of two characters and a text format of uppercase.
   c. Insert a text form field for *Zip Code:* that specifies a maximum length of five characters.
   d. Insert a text form field for *Medical Insurance:* that specifies *Premiere Group* as the default text.
   e. Insert a check box form field in the cell immediately left of *Both parents* that is marked with an *X* by default.
   f. Insert a text form field for the first *Relationship:* that specifies *Mother* as the default text.
   g. Insert a text form field for the second *Relationship:* that specifies *Father* as the default text.
   h. Insert the remaining text and check box form fields as shown in Figure WB-4.2.
3. Protect the template to allow only filling in the form.
4. Save and then close **4-WCDSForm.dotx**.

Figure WB-4.2 Assessment 2

5. Use File Explorer to create a form document from the template
   4-WCDSForm.dotx and then insert the following data in the specified fields:

   Patient Name: Ethan Mark Springer
   Patient Number: 4221
   Address: 345 Jackson Court
   City: Bismarck
   State: nd (This text will change to uppercase when the Tab key is pressed.)
   Zip Code: 58506
   Telephone: (701) 555-3481
   Medical Insurance: (Leave the default *Premiere Group*.)
   (Leave the *X* in the *Both parents* check box.)
   Relationship: (Leave the default *Mother*.)
   Relationship: (Leave the default *Father*.)
   Name: Elizabeth Springer
   Name: Chris Springer
   Address: 345 Jackson Court, Bismarck, ND 58506
   Address: 345 Jackson Court, Bismarck, ND 58506

Home Telephone: (701) 555-3481
Home Telephone: (701) 555-3481
Work Telephone: (701) 555-8711
Work Telephone: (701) 555-0075

6. Save the document with the name **4-WCDSSpringer**.
7. Print and then close **4-WCDSSpringer.docx**.

Create and Fill in a Contact Request Form

1. At a blank document, create the form document shown in Figure WB-4.3 with the following specifications:
   a. Create a table with the rows and columns shown in the figure.
   b. Set the company name, address, and form title in Copperplate Gothic Bold (the symbol in the address is located in the Wingdings font, character code 177) and the remaining text in Calibri. (You determine the font sizes.)
   c. Insert text form fields for the first five fields.
   d. Insert check box form fields for the fields in the middle section.
   e. For the question on how the representative should contact the respondent, insert a drop-down form field with the choices *Email*, *Phone*, and *Mail*. For the question on how the respondent learned about Northland Security Systems, insert a drop-down form field with the choices *Internet*, *Colleague*, *Friend*, *Yellow Pages*.
   f. Apply additional formatting to the form document so it appears similar to the one shown in Figure WB-4.3.
2. Save the completed form document as a template with the name **4-NSSForm** to the WL3C4 folder on your storage medium.

Figure WB-4.3 Assessment 3

3. Use File Explorer to create a form document from the template **4-NSSForm.dotx** and then fill in each form field with data of your choosing.
4. Save the completed document with the name **4-NSSDoc**.
5. Print and then close **4-NSSDoc.docx**.

Assessment 4

Data Files

Create and Fill in a Dental Referral Form

1. The forms used in this chapter contain the form data in a table. While using a table facilitates displaying information in an organized and logical manner, it is not necessary when creating a form. Open **WCDSLtrhd.docx** and then create a referral form (without using a table) with the following information. (You determine the appropriate form fields to insert in the form.)
   - Referral date
   - Patient's name, address, city, state, and zip code
   - Patient's date of birth
   - Home phone
   - Cell phone
   - Email
   - Dental insurance
   - Referring dentist
   - Reason for referral (include the following in a drop-down list: *Periodontal evaluation*, *Implant consultation*, and *Emergency care*)
   - Comments
2. Save the completed document as a template with the name **4-WCDSReferral** in the WL3C4 folder on your storage medium.
3. Use File Explorer to create a form document from the template **4-WCDSReferral.dotx** and then fill in each form field with data of your choosing.
4. Save the completed document with the name **4-WCDSDoc**.
5. Print and then close **4-WCDSDoc.docx**.

Visual Benchmark

Data Files

Create and Fill in a Secondary Payer Form

1. Create the template and form fields shown in Figure WB-4.4 with the following specifications:
   a. Consider using **ERCFundApp.docx** to help you create the form shown in Figure WB-4.4. (Make sure the gridlines display.)
   b. Insert form fields and apply formatting similar to what is shown in Figure WB-4.4.
   c. Consider specifying text form field options for the *State:* and *Zip Code:* form fields.
2. Save the document as a template with the name **4-ERCInsForm** in the WL3C4 folder on your storage medium.
3. Protect the template to allow only filling in the form without setting a password.
4. Save and then close **4-ERCInsForm.dotx**.
5. Use File Explorer to create a form document based on the template **4-ERCInsForm.dotx** and then insert data of your choosing in each form field.
6. Save the document with the name **4-ERCInsDoc**.
7. Print and then close **4-ERCInsDoc.docx**.

Figure WB-4.4 Visual Benchmark

Evergreen Regional Center

9800 Vineville Avenue ◈ Macon, GA 31206 ◈ (478) 555-9800

SECONDARY PAYER FORM

Patient Name: ▭   Patient Number: ▭

Address: ▭   City: ▭   State: ▭   Zip Code: ▭

Telephone: ▭   Date of Birth: ▭

Please answer the following questions related to your illness or injury:

Yes	No	
☐	☐	Is illness/injury due to an automobile accident?
☐	☐	Is illness/injury due to an accident covered by Worker's Compensation?
☐	☐	Does the Black Lung Program cover this illness?
☐	☐	Are you eligible for coverage under the Veterans Administration?
☐	☐	If under 65, do you have Medicare coverage due to a disability?
☐	☐	Do you have coverage under a spouse's health insurance plan?

Name of Insurance Company: ▭   Telephone Number: ▭

Name of Policy Holder: ▭   Policy Number: ▭

Case Study

Part

1

Data Files

You are the owner of Impressions Art Gallery and need to create forms for this business. Open **IAGLtrhd.docx** and then save it as a template with the name **4-IAGConsignForm** in the WL3C4 folder on your storage medium. Create an artwork consignment form in a table that includes the following information (you determine the formatting of the information, the form fields, and any form field options that are appropriate):

- Current date
- Artist's name
- Name of artwork
- Price
- Start date of consignment
- End date of consignment
- Gallery commission percentage
- Include a location in the form for the gallery owner's signature (use your name) and the artist's signature

Use File Explorer to create a form document from the template **4-IAGConsignForm.dotx** and then insert data of your choosing in each field. Save the document with the name **4-IAGConsign**. Print and then close **4-IAGConsign.docx**.

Part

2

Data Files

Create an artist application form for Impressions Art Gallery (begin with the document **IAGLtrhd.docx** and save the form as a template with the name **4-IAGAppForm** in the WL3C4 folder on your storage medium) that includes the following (you determine the formatting, form fields, and any form field options):

- Name
- Street address, city, state, and zip code
- Home phone
- Cell phone
- Email
- Website
- Education (art degree, private workshops, college art classes, self-taught)
- Years as an artist
- Art style (realism, abstract, expressionistic, impressionistic)
- Art media
    - Painting/drawing (acrylic, collage, charcoal, ink, mixed-media, oil, pastels, other)
    - Photography (digital, film, black and white, montage/collage)

Use File Explorer to create a form document from the template **4-IAGAppForm.dotx** and then insert data of your choosing in each field. Save the document with the name **4-IAGArtistApp**. Print and then close **4-IAGArtistApp.docx**.

Part 3

For some art sales, Impressions Art Gallery ships the artwork to the client's business or home. Create a shipping form that includes the information needed to identify the client, the artist, the artwork, and other pertinent information (such as the current date, shipping date, shipping method, and so on). You determine the specific data and form fields for the form. Begin with the document **IAGLtrhd.docx** and save it as a template with the name **4-IAG-ShipForm** in the WL3C4 folder on your storage medium. After completing, saving, and closing the template, use File Explorer to create a form document from the template and then insert data of your choosing in each field. Save the document with the name **4-IAGShipping**. Print and then close **4-IAGShipping.docx**.

Part 4

You are planning an art exhibit at Impressions Art Gallery from June 1 to June 30, 2018, and want to create an artist exhibit application form to be completed by an artist interested in showing his or her work at the exhibit. Search online using the keywords *artist exhibit application* and then review several different application examples. After reviewing examples, open **IAGLtrhd.docx** and then create an artist exhibit application form that contains only the pertinent information. (You do not need to include any legal language.) Save the form as a template with the name **4-IAGExhibitForm** in the WL3C4 folder on your storage medium and then close the template. Use File Explorer to create a form document from the template and then insert data of your choosing in each field. Save the document with the name **4-IAGExhibitApp**. Print and then close **4-IAGExhibitApp.docx**.

Part 5

In the future, your assistant will create any additional forms needed for Impressions Art Gallery. To help the assistant understand how you designed and formatted the current forms, you decide to create a document that describes how you formatted the **4-IAGConsignForm** template, the form fields you used in the template, and the form field options you applied to the fields. Include any additional information you think will be helpful to the assistant. Save the completed document with the name **4-IAGForms**. Print and then close **4-IAGForms.docx**.

Using Outline View and Creating a Table of Authorities

Study Tools

Study tools include a presentation and a list of chapter Quick Steps and Hint margin notes. Use these resources to help you further develop and review skills learned in this chapter.

Concepts Check

Check your understanding by identifying application tools used in this chapter. If you are a SNAP user, launch the Concepts Check from your Assignments page.

Recheck

Check your understanding by taking this quiz. If you are a SNAP user, launch the Recheck from your Assignments page.

Skills Exercise

Additional activities are available to SNAP users. If you are a SNAP user, access these activities from your Assignments page.

Skills Assessment

Assessment

1

Data Files

Assign Levels in Outline View

1. Open **EmpComp.docx** and then save it with the name **5-EmpComp**.
2. Change to Outline view and then promote or demote titles and headings as follows:

> *COMPENSATION*: Level 1
> *Rate of Pay*: Level 2
> *Pay Progression*: Level 2
> *Overtime*: Level 2
> *Shift Differential*: Level 2
> *EMPLOYEE PERFORMANCE*: Level 1
> *Work Performance Standards*: Level 2
> *Performance Evaluation*: Level 2
> *Employment Records*: Level 2

3. Collapse the outline so only the two levels of titles and headings display.
4. Save and then print **5-EmpComp.docx**. (This will print the collapsed outline, not the entire document.)

Move and Delete Headings in a Collapsed Outline

1. With **5-EmpComp.docx** open, make sure the document displays in Outline view and then save it with the name **5-EmpComp2**.
2. Make the following changes to the document:
   a. Use the *Show Level* option box to show only level 1 headings in the outline.
   b. Move the title *COMPENSATION* below the title *EMPLOYEE PERFORMANCE*.
   c. Use the *Show Level* option box to show level 2 headings (and level 1 headings).
   d. Move the heading *Pay Progression* below the heading *Overtime*.
   e. Delete the *Shift Differential* heading.
3. Do not show text formatting.
4. Save and then print **5-EmpComp2.docx**.
5. Display the entire document and then close Outline view.
6. Save and then close **5-EmpComp2.docx**.

Assign Levels at the Paragraph Dialog Box

1. Open **WritingProcess.docx** and then save it with the name **5-WritingProcess**.
2. Using options at the Paragraph dialog box, assign level 1 to the titles *THE WRITING PROCESS* and *REFERENCES* (located on page 3) and assign level 2 to the seven headings in the document.
3. Collapse the body text below the heading *Identify Reader* and then collapse the body text below the heading *Define Purpose*. Select the heading *Define Purpose* and then use the mouse to drag the selected heading to the beginning of the heading *Identify Reader*.
4. Print page 1 of the document.
5. Expand the body text below the heading *Define Purpose* and then expand the body text below the heading *Identify Reader*.
6. Specify that the title *THE WRITING PROCESS* should open collapsed by default and then specify that the title *REFERENCES* should open collapsed by default.
7. Save and then close **5-WritingProcess.docx**.
8. Open, print, and then close **5-WritingProcess.docx**.

Create and Arrange a Master Document

1. Open **WebContent.docx** and then save it with the name **5-WebContent**.
2. Change to Outline view.
3. Assign level 1 to the following headings:

   Browsing Web Pages
   Searching Online Content
   Evaluating Web Content
   Intellectual Property

4. Click the Show Document button in the Master Document group on the Outlining tab.
5. Create subdocuments by selecting the entire document and then clicking the Create button in the Master Document group.
6. Save and then close **5-WebContent.docx**.

7. Open **5-WebContent.docx** and then edit a subdocument by completing the following steps:
   a. Open the subdocument **Searching Online Content.docx**.
   b. Delete the last paragraph.
   c. Save, print, and then close the subdocument.
8. Display the document in Outline view, delete the **Evaluating Web Content.docx** subdocument, and then close Outline view.
9. Save, print, and then close **5-WebContent.docx**.

Assessment

5

Data Files

Create a Table of Authorities for a Legal Brief

1. Open **SilversBrief.docx** and then save it with the name **5-SilversBrief**.
2. Mark the following as case citations with the specified short citations. *Hint: Use the Find feature to help you locate each citation.*
   a. *Richmond Newspapers, Inc. v. Virginia*, 448 U.S. 555 (1983) Short citation: Richmond Newspapers, Inc. v. Virginia
   b. *Globe Newspaper Co. v. Superior Court*, 457 U.S. 596 (1985) Short citation: Globe Newspaper Co. v. Superior Court
   c. *Naucke v. City of Park Hills*, 284 F. 3d 923, 927 (2d Cir. 2005) Short citation: Naucke v. City of Park Hills
   d. *Singer v. Fulton County Sheriff*, 63 F. 3d 110, 120 (2d Cir. 1998) Short citation: Singer v. Fulton County Sheriff
   e. *Bowden v. Keane*, 237 F. 3d 125, 129 (2d Cir. 2004) Short citation: Bowden v. Keane
   f. *Cf. Guzman v. Scully*, 80 F. 3d 772, 775-76 (2d Cir. 1999) Short citation: Cf. Guzman v. Scully
3. Press Ctrl + Home to move the insertion point to the beginning of the document and then press the Enter key.
4. With the insertion point positioned at the beginning of *STATEMENT OF CASE*, insert a section break that begins a new page.
5. With the insertion point positioned below the section break, insert a page number at the bottom center of each page and change the starting number to 1.
6. Move the insertion point to the beginning of the document, type TABLE OF AUTHORITIES, and center and apply bold formatting to the heading.
7. Press the Enter key, turn off bold formatting, and change the paragraph alignment back to left.
8. Insert a table of authorities. (You determine the format style.)
9. With the insertion point positioned in the table of authorities, change the page numbering format to lowercase roman numerals.
10. Save, print, and then close **5-SilversBrief.docx**.

Figure WB-5.1 Visual Benchmark, Part 1

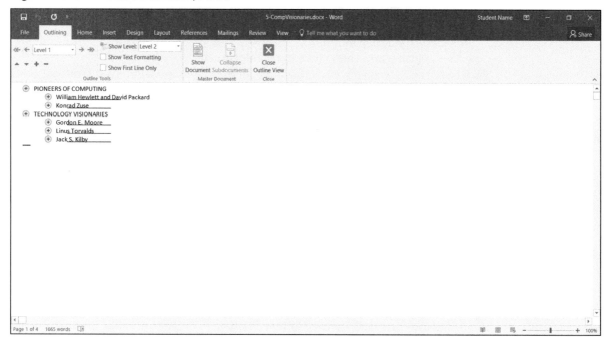

Visual Benchmark

Part 1

Assign Levels and Rearrange Text in a Computer Visionaries Document

Data Files

1. Open **CompVisionaries.docx** and then save it with the name **5-CompVisionaries**.
2. Display the document in Outline view and then assign levels and rearrange the titles and headings (and the body text below each heading) so your outline matches the one in Figure WB-5.1.
3. Save and then print **5-CompVisionaries.docx**.
4. Display the entire document and then close Outline view.
5. Save and then close **5-CompVisionaries.docx**.

Part 2

Create a Master Document and Subdocuments

Data Files

1. Open **BuildWebsite.docx** and then save it with the name **5-BuildWebsite**.
2. Use **5-BuildWebsite.docx** along with **HostWebsite.docx** and **OrganizeWebsite.docx** to create the master document and subdocuments shown in Figure WB-5.2.
3. With the master document displayed in Outline view, collapse the subdocuments and then close Outline view.
4. Save and then print **5-BuildWebsite.docx**. (Print the document with the subdocuments collapsed.)
5. Close **5-BuildWebsite.docx**.

Figure WB-5.2 Visual Benchmark, Part 2

BUILDING A WEBSITE

A website consists of pages that may contain text, graphics, animation, audio files, movies, links to other pages and sites, forms for entering information into databases, and other materials. Pages are created using the Hypertext Markup Language (HTML), a script language that also allows many "embedded" languages such as Java or Visual Basic too run within it. Using HTML, script, or code, to create web pages offers some special advantages. Unlike the code in software that people buy at a retail outlet, the source code of web pages is transmitted to users' computers when they navigate to a URL. Downloading the HTML source code for an existing page and copying the format of the page is legal as long as you change its content. However, most people consider copying the work of others without crediting the original developer as "bad form." A second advantage of using a script language such as HTML is that it greatly reduces the size of file that needs to be transmitted, and thereby decreases the amount of time required to display the page on the user's screen.

F:\WL3C5\Planning a Website.docx

F:\WL3C5\Choosing a Host.docx

F:\WL3C5\Free Hosting Services.docx

F:\WL3C5\Hosting from ISPs.docx

F:\WL3C5\Paid Hosting Services.docx

F:\WL3C5\Organizing the Site.docx

Case Study

Part 1

Data Files

You are an administrative assistant for Northland Security Systems and the training coordinator has asked you to edit a document on computer devices. Open **NSSCompDevices.docx** and then save it with the name **5-NSSCompDevices**. The training coordinator wants you to assign levels to the titles and headings in the document (but not apply styles). In addition, he wants you to specify that the three titles in the document should open collapsed by default. Save the edited document and then close it. Open **5-NSSCompDevices.docx**. The training coordinator wants you to rearrange the document so the *Computer Output Devices* title and information displays first, the *Computer Input Devices* title and information displays second, and the *Computer Keyboards* title and information displays third. Save the rearranged document, print the collapsed document, and then close it.

Part 2

Data Files

The Human Resources Department manager at Northland Security Systems has asked you to compile an employee handbook as a master document with a number of subdocuments. Open **NSSHandbook.docx** and then save it with the name **5-NSSHandbook**. Insert **NSSSection1.docx, NSSSection2.docx, NSSSection3.docx**, and **NSSSection4.docx** at the end of the document. Display the document in Outline view, assign level 1 to the title *Employee Handbook*; level 2 to the section 1, section 2, section 3, and section 4 headings (the section headings that display in all capital letters); and level 3 to the headings below all the sections. Do not assign levels to the outline text in the *Employee Handbook* section. Create subdocuments with the level 2 headings and body text. Save the completed master document, print the document with the subdocuments collapsed, and then close **5-NSSHandbook.docx**.

Part

3

After reviewing the master document **5-NSSHandbook.docx** that you created for Northland Security Systems, your supervisor has asked you to edit some of the subdocuments. She has asked you to edit the section 1 subdocument by deleting the *Security* heading and the body text that follows the heading and then rearranging the information in the subdocument so it appears in this order:

NEW EMPLOYEE ORIENTATION

INTRODUCTORY PERIOD

PERFORMANCE REVIEW

MEDICAL SCREENINGS

LICENSURE

IDENTIFICATION BADGES

Edit the section 2 subdocument so that the employee communication information appears after the employer communication information. Make changes to the outline below the title *Employee Handbook* so the changes you made are reflected in the outline text. (Make sure each heading displays with 6 points of spacing after paragraphs.) After making the edits, save, print, and then close **5-NSSHandbook.docx**. Open, print, and then close the section 1 subdocument and then the section 2 subdocument.

Part

4

Data Files

The Training Department at Northland Security Systems provides an instructional manual for employees that includes information on using Word, Excel, PowerPoint, and Access features. The Training Department manager has asked you to create a document that provides information on creating a master document. Open **NSSLtrhd.docx** and then save it with the name **5-NSSMasterDoc**. Type information in the document that provides information and instructions on how to create a master document and subdocuments. Provide as much detail as possible and apply formatting so the document is attractive and easy to read. Save the completed document and then print and close it.

Sharing Documents and Customizing Word Options

Skills Exercise

Skills Assessment

Assessment

1

Data Files

Improve the Accessibility of a Document

1. Open **WebReport.docx** and then save it with the name **6-WebReport**.
2. Apply the Heading 1 style to the two titles in the document.
3. Apply the Heading 2 style to the four headings in the document.
4. Apply the Basic (Stylish) style set.
5. Apply the Blue Green theme colors.
6. Run an accessibility check on the document and then make the following corrections:
   a. Provide alternate text for the image (Picture 4) with a title of *Globe* and a description of *Globe with www letters*.
   b. Provide alternate text for the first table with a title of *Domain Suffixes* and a description of *Common top-level domain suffixes*.
   c. Provide alternate text for the second table with a title of *Search Tools* and a description of *Common search tools*.
   d. Delete the blank row in the first table.
   e. Delete the extra blank characters.
   f. Remove the watermark.
7. Modify the Heading 1 style so it applies bold formatting.
8. Modify the Heading 2 style so it applies bold formatting and changes the font size to 16 points.
9. Save, print, and then close **6-WebReport.docx**.

Share a Document

Note: To complete this optional project, you need to be connected to the Internet and have a OneDrive account.

1. Open **6-WebReport.docx** and then save it to your OneDrive account and name it **6-WebReport-Shared**.
2. With **6-WebReport-Shared.docx** open, display the Share backstage area with the *Share with People* option selected and then click the Share with People button.
3. Type the email address for your instructor in the *Invite people* text box in the Share task pane.
4. Specify that the document can be viewed but not edited and then click the Share button.
5. Check to determine if your instructor received the email.
6. Close the Share task pane and then close **6-WebReport-Shared.docx**.

Present a Document Online

1. Open **6-WebReport.docx** and then save it with the name **6-WebReport-Online**.
2. Display the Share backstage area, click the *Present Online* option, and then click the Present Online button.
3. At the Present Online window, click the CONNECT button. If a CONNECT button does not display, skip to Step 5.
4. Type your user name and password in the Windows Security dialog box.
5. Click the <u>Copy Link</u> hyperlink.
6. Send the link to your instructor or a colleague by opening the desired email account, pasting the link into a new message window, and then sending the email.
7. When the link has been received by your instructor or colleague, click the START PRESENTATION button in the Present Online window.
8. Select and then delete the second row in Table A (the row that displays *.biz* in the first column). Resume the presentation.
9. End the online presentation of the document.
10. If necessary, increase the zoom of the document back to 100%.
11. Save, print, and then close **6-WebReport-Online.docx**.

Data Files

Customize Word Options

1. With Word open, press Ctrl + N to open a blank document.
2. Display the Word Options dialog box with *General* selected in the left panel.
3. Change the Office background to Calligraphy and the Office theme to White and then click OK to close the dialog box so the changes take effect.
4. Display the Word Options dialog box with *General* selected in the left panel and then complete the following steps:
   a. Drag the dialog box to the right so the left side of the page is visible.
   b. Press the Print Screen button to make a screen capture of the entire screen.
   c. Close the Word Options dialog box.
   d. Click the Paste button. (This inserts the screen capture image in the document.)
   e. Press Ctrl + End and then press the Enter key.
5. Display the Word Options dialog box with *General* selected in the left panel and then return the Office background to No Background and the Office theme to Colorful.
6. Click *Display* in the left panel, specify that white space between pages in Print Layout view should not display, and then click OK to close the dialog box.

7. Display the Word Options dialog box with *Display* selected in the left panel.
8. Complete steps similar to those in Steps 4a through 4e to insert a screen capture image of the screen.
9. Open **TTSHawaii.docx** and then save it with the name **6-TTSHawaii**.
10. Display the Word Options dialog box with *Display* selected and then specify that white space between pages in Print Layout view should display.
11. Click *Advanced* in the left panel, specify that background colors and images should not display in Print Layout and that text boundaries should display (both options are located in the *Show document content* section), and then click OK to close the dialog box.
12. Display the Word Options dialog box with *Advanced* selected and then display the section of the dialog box in which the changes were made.
13. If necessary, drag the dialog box to the right so the left side of the page is visible and then press the Print Screen key.
14. Click OK to close the Word Options dialog box.
15. Close **6-TTSHawaii.docx**.
16. At the document containing the screen capture images, click the Paste button and then press the Enter key.
17. Display the Word Options dialog box with *Advanced* selected, specify that background colors and images should display in Print Layout and that text boundaries should not display (both options are located in the *Show document content* section), and then click OK to close the dialog box.
18. Display the Account backstage area and then make a screen capture of the screen.
19. Close the Account backstage area and then paste the image in the document.
20. Scroll through the document and make sure all four images display on two pages and that the same amount of space displays between the images.
21. Save the document and name it **6-WordOptionsImages**.
22. Print and then close **6-WordOptionsImages.docx**.

Visual Benchmark

Improve the Accessibility of a Document

Part

1

Data Files ▶

1. Open **PremPro.docx** and then save it with the name **6-PremPro**.
2. Format the document so it appears similar to what is shown in Figure WB-6.1 with the following specifications:
   a. Apply the Heading 1 style to the title and the Heading 2 style to the headings.
   b. Apply the Organic theme and the Green theme colors.
   c. Modify the Heading 1 style so it centers the text, applies bold formatting, and changes the font size to 24 points.
   d. Modify the Heading 2 style so it applies bold formatting and changes the font size to 16 points.
   e. Modify the Body Text style so it changes the font size to 14 points. (Refer to Project 1, Step 12.)
3. Run an accessibility check on the document and then make the following corrections:
   a. Provide alternate text for the table and the diagram (the SmartArt graphic). You determine the title and description for the table and for the diagram.)
   b. Specify a header row for the table. (Do this at the Table Properties dialog box with the Row tab selected.)
   c. Delete the blank row in the table.
   d. Specify that the diagram should wrap in line with the text.

Premium Produce

Farm-Fresh and Organic Produce

Premium Produce is your source for local, farm-fresh produce. All of our produce is organically grown without pesticides, herbicides, and other sprays. We ship our produce daily to a six-state region in the West.

Featured Produce of the Month

Many fruits and vegetables are being harvested now while they are at the peak of their flavor. Featured produce for this month includes:

Fruit	Vegetable
Red Delicious apples	Acorn squash
Mandarin oranges	Russet potatoes
Lemons	Vidalia onions

Ordering from Premium Produce

Before ordering from Premium Produce, check our sale prices for the current month by visiting our website at www.emcp.net/prempro. At our website, click the <u>Pricing</u> link that displays in the upper right corner of the window. After viewing the sale prices, call our toll-free number at 1-800-555-8900.

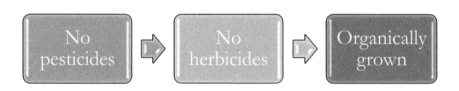

4. Save **6-PremPro.docx**.
5. Press the Print Screen button to make a screen capture of **6-PremPro.docx** (with the Accessibility Checker task pane open).
6. Press Ctrl + N to open a blank document and then paste the screen capture into the document.
7. Save the document containing the screen capture and name it **6-PremProScreencap**.
8. Print and then close **6-PremProScreencap.docx**.
9. At **6-PremPro.docx**, close the Accessibility Checker task pane.
10. Save, print, and then close **6-PremPro.docx**.

Part 2

Customize Word Options and Insert Screen Captures

1. Open **RepAgrmnt.docx** and then save it with the name **6-RepAgrmnt**.
2. Make changes at the Word Options dialog box, as shown in Figure WB-6.2, and make a screen capture that matches what is shown in the figure.
3. Press Ctrl + N to open a blank document and then insert the screen capture image into it.
4. Press Ctrl + End and then press the Enter key two times.
5. Save the document and name it **6-ScreenCaptures**.
6. Make **6-RepAgrmnt.docx** active; make changes at the Word Options dialog box, as shown in Figure WB-6.3; and make a screen capture that matches what is shown in the figure.
7. Make **6-ScreenCaptures.docx** active and then insert the screen capture image into it.
8. Make any other adjustments so your document appears similar to what is shown in the figure.
9. Save, print, and then close **6-ScreenCaptures.docx**.
10. Return the Word Options back to the default settings.
11. Save and then close **6-RepAgrmnt.docx**.

Figure WB-6.2 Visual Benchmark, Part 2, Step 2

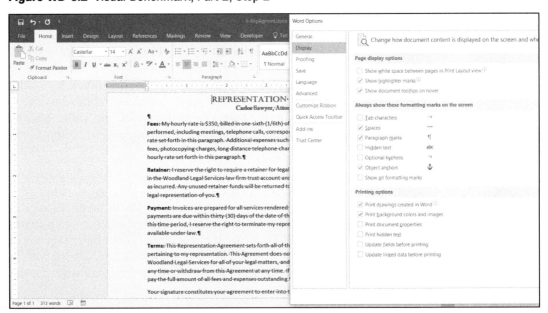

Figure WB-6.3 Visual Benchmark, Part 2, Step 6

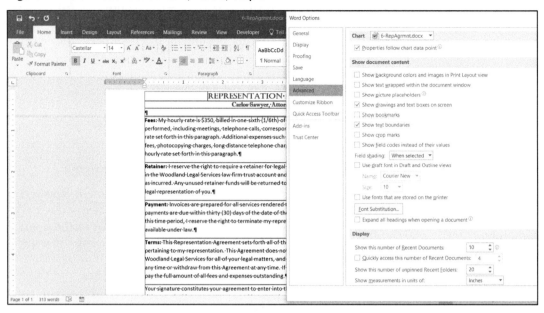

Case Study

As the office manager for Tandem Energy Corporation, you need to ensure that company documents are accessible to employees and clients with visual impairments. Open **TECTables.docx** and then save it with the name **6-TECTables**. Run an accessibility check on the document and make all the necessary changes to make the document accessible. Before closing the Accessibility Checker task pane, make a screen capture of the entire screen and then paste it into a blank document. Save the document with the screen capture and name it **6-TSPScreenCap**. Print and then close **6-TSPScreenCap.docx**. With **6-TSPTables.docx** open, close the Accessibility Checker task pane and then save, print, and close the document.

Open **TECRpt.docx** and then save it with the name **6-TECRpt**. Apply heading styles to the title and headings in the document. Run an accessibility check on the document and correct any issues displayed in the Accessibility Checker task pane. To improve the readability of the document for someone with a visual impairment, edit the styles applied to the title and headings so the font sizes are larger. Also increase the font size of the Body Text style. After making the changes, save, print, and then close **6-TECRpt.docx**.

Anita Seidel, the Human Resources Department manager at Tandem Energy Corporation, would like to review the document **6-TECRpt** that has been checked for accessibility issues and wants you to send it to her as an email attachment. (You will be sending the email with the document attached to your instructor.) Open **6-TECRpt.docx** and then use options at the Share backstage area to send an email to your instructor with **6-TECRpt.docx** attached. Check with your instructor to determine whether he or she received the email with the document attached.

Part 3

As the office manager for Tandem Energy Corporation, you decide to keep track of the Word account information and product identification number by creating screen captures and saving them in a document. Make a screen capture of the Account backstage area and paste the image in a blank document. Display the Account backstage area, click the About Word button, and then make a screen capture of the information that displays. Paste the image into the document below the first image. Make any necessary adjustments to the two images so they display on one page. Save the document and name it **6-TECAcctInfo**. Print and then close **6-TECAcctInfo.docx**.

Part 4

Word options for all the computers at Tandem Energy Corporation will be standardized and as the office manager, you need to create a document with the steps for making the changes. Create a document that provides the steps to complete the following changes:

- Apply the Dark Gray office theme.
- Turn on the display of tab characters and hidden text.
- Change the number of minutes to five minutes for saving AutoRecover information.
- Change the number of recent documents that displays in the *Recent* option list to 25 documents.

Save the completed document and name it **6-TECOptionsSteps**. Print and then close **6-TECOptionsSteps.docx**.

Microsoft® Word Level 3

Performance Assessment

Assessing Proficiency

In the previous chapters, you have learned how to apply advanced character formatting, find and replace fonts and special characters, create and manage macros and styles, create forms with content controls and legacy tools, create master documents and subdocuments, create a table of authorities, improve the accessibility of documents, share documents, and customize Word options.

Assessment

1

Data Files

Apply Character Spacing and OpenType Features

1. Open **CVTakeoutMenu.docx** and then save it with the name **U-CVTakeoutMenu**.
2. Select the title *Take Out Menu*, change the character spacing to Expanded by 1.5 points, turn on kerning, apply Stylistic Set 5, and use contextual alternates. (Do this at the Font dialog box with the Advanced tab selected.)
3. Select the heading *Soups*, change the font size to 22 points, change the character spacing to Expanded by 1 point, turn on kerning, and apply Stylistic Set 5.
4. Apply the same formatting applied to the heading *Soups* in Step 3 to the other headings (*Salads*, *Main Dishes*, and *Desserts*).
5. Select the last sentence in the document (the sentence that begins *Enjoy the tastes*) and then turn on kerning and apply Stylistic Set 5.
6. Save, print, and then close **U-CVTakeoutMenu.docx**.

Assessment

2

Data Files

Find and Replace Formatting and Use a Wildcard Character

1. Open **Agreement.docx** and then save it with the name **U-Agreement**.
2. Find text set in the *+Headings* font and replace the font with Corbel.
3. Find text set in the *+Body* font and replace the font with Candara.
4. Using a wildcard character, find all occurrences of *Pin?h?rst?Mad?s?n Builders* and replace them with *Pinehurst-Madisen Builders*. (Make sure you remove the formatting option from the *Find what* and *Replace with* text boxes.)

5. Using a wildcard character, find all occurrences of *?erry L?w?ndowsk?* and replace them with *Gerry Lewandowski*.

6. Save, print, and then close **U-Agreement.docx**.

<table>
<tr><td>

Assessment

3

Data Files

</td><td>

Insert Fields in a Main Document and Merge with an Excel File

1. Open **MAMD.docx** and then save it with the name **U-MAMD**. (At the message indicating that opening the document will run the SQL command, click Yes.)

2. Specify the Excel file **MACustomers.xlsx** as the data source file.

3. Insert the address and greeting line fields in the appropriate locations in the document.

4. Position the insertion point immediately right of the period that ends the first sentence in the second paragraph and then press the spacebar. Insert an If...Then...Else... field that tells Word to insert the sentence *If you buy a new car from us, we will offer you top trade-in dollars for your used car.* if the plan is equal to *Purchase* or otherwise inserts the sentence *We are offering incredible deals on leased automobiles and upgrades to newer models.*

5. Replace the *XX* near the end of the letter with your initials.

6. Position the insertion point on the blank line below your initials, type Letter, press the spacebar, and then insert a Merge Record # field.

7. Save **U-MAMD.docx** and then merge the main document with the Excel data source file.

8. Save the merged document with the name **U-MALetters**.

9. Print and then close **U-MALetters.docx**.

10. Save and then close **U-MAMD.docx**.

</td></tr>
<tr><td>

Assessment

4

Data Files

</td><td>

Create and Run Macros

1. Open **APMMacros.docm** (which is a macro-enabled document) and then save it with the name **U-APMMacros**. (Make sure it is saved as a macro-enabled document with the *.docm* file extension.)

2. Create a macro named APMFormat that is saved in **U-APMMacros.docm** (change the *Store macro in* option to *U-APMMacros.docm (document)*) that selects the entire entire document (use Ctrl + A), changes the font to Constantia and the font color to standard dark blue, and then deselects the text. (Make the changes to the font and font color at the Font dialog box.)

3. Position the insertion point at the beginning of the text *Title text* and then create a macro named APMTitle (saved in **U-APMMacros.docm**) that selects the title text (press the F8 function key and then press the End key); changes the font to 14 points; applies bold formatting; centers the text; applies Blue, Accent 1, Lighter 60% shading (fifth column, third row in the *Theme Colors* section); and deselects the text.

4. Press Ctrl + End and then create a macro named APMInfo (saved in **U-APMMacros.docm**) that includes the information shown in Figure WB-U.1. Insert Fill-in fields in the macro in place of the name and date in parentheses.

5. After recording the macros, select and then delete all the text in the document.

6. Save **U-APMMacros.docm**.

7. Save the document with the name **U-APMLease**. (Make sure it is saved as a macro-enabled document with the *.docm* file extension.)

8. Insert **Lease.docx** into the document. (Do this with the Object button on the Insert tab.)

</td></tr>
</table>

Figure WB-U.1 Assessment 4

This document is the sole property of Azure Property Management and may not be reproduced, copied, or sold without express written consent of a legal representative of Azure Property Management. *(press Enter)*

Prepared by: (name) *(press Shift + Enter)*
Date: (date)

9. Move the insertion point to the beginning of the document and then run the APMFormat macro.
10. Position the insertion point at the beginning of the title *LEASE AGREEMENT* and then run the APMTitle macro.
11. Move the insertion point to the end of the document and then run the APMInfo macro. Insert the following information when prompted:

    (name) Grace Hillstrand
    (date) October 25, 2018

12. Save, print, and then close **U-APMLease.docm**.
13. Open **U-APMMacros.docm** and if a security warning displays, click the Enable Content button. If a warning displays asking if you want to make the first a trusted document, click Yes.
14. Save the document with the name **U-APMREAgrmnt**. (Make sure it is saved with the *.docm* file extension.)
15. Insert **REAgrmnt.docx** into the document. (Do this with the Object button on the Insert tab.)
16. Move the insertion point to the beginning of the document and then run the APMFormat macro.
17. With the insertion point positioned at the beginning of the title *REAL ESTATE SALE AGREEMENT*, run the APMTitle macro.
18. Move the insertion point to the end of the document and then run the APMInfo macro. Insert the following information when prompted:

    (name) Grace Hillstrand
    (date) October 28, 2018

19. Save, print, and then close **U-APMREAgrmnt.docm**.

Assessment 5

Data Files

Create and Apply Styles to a Business Document

1. Open **TRStyles.docx** and then save it with the name **U-TRStyles**.
2. Create a style based on the formatting of the *Title* text and name it TRTitle. (Make sure you select the paragraph symbol with the text.)
3. Create a style based on the formatting of the *Heading 1* text and name it TRHeading1.
4. Create a style based on the formatting of the *Heading 2* text and name it TRHeading2.
5. Click in the first cell in the blank table and then create a table style with the following specifications:
   a. Display the Create New Style from Formatting dialog box and then type TRTable as the style name.
   b. Click the Modify button and then change the *Style type* option to *Table*.

c. With *Whole table* selected in the *Apply formatting to* option, change the font to Corbel and the font size to 12 points.

d. Use the Border button to apply all borders to the table.

e. Change the *Apply formatting to* option to *Header row*.

f. Change the font size to 14 points, apply bold formatting, and apply the Light Gray, Background 2, Darker 75% fill color (third column, fifth row in the *Theme Colors* section).

g. Change the *Apply formatting to* option to *Even banded rows* and then apply the Gold, Accent 4, Lighter 40% fill color (eighth column, fourth row in the *Theme Colors* section).

h. Click OK to close the Create New Style from Formatting dialog box.

6. Press Ctrl + End to move the insertion point to the end of the document and then create a new style named TRSlogan. Apply the following formatting at the Create New Style from Formatting expanded dialog box:

a. Display the Paragraph dialog box (click the Format button in the lower left corner of the dialog box and then click *Paragraph*), change to center alignment, the left and right indents to 1.5 inch, the spacing after paragraphs to 3 points, and the line spacing to single spacing. Click OK to close the dialog box.

b. Display the Borders and Shading dialog box (click the Format button and then click *Border*), change the border width to 2¼ points, and then apply top and bottom borders. Click OK to close the dialog box.

c. Click the Bold button and then the Italic button.

d. Click OK to close the Create New Style from Formatting dialog box.

7. Save the styles you created in a style set named with your three initials followed by *TRentals*.

8. Save and then close **U-TRStyles.docx**.

9. Open **TRBusCode.docx** and then save it with the name **U-TRBusCode**.

10. Change to the style set named with your initials followed by *TRentals*.

11. Apply the TRTitle style to the title *Business Conduct Code*.

12. Apply the TRHeading1 style to the six headings in the report (the headings in all uppercase letters).

13. Apply the TRHeading2 style to the five subheadings in the report (the subheadings with only the first letter of each word capitalized).

14. Move the insertion point to the end of the document, select the last two lines of text, and then apply the TRSlogan style to the selected text.

15. Edit the TRHeading1 style by changing the font size to 12 points and the font color to Light Gray, Background 2, Darker 75% (third column, fifth row in the *Theme Colors* section).

16. Turn on the display of the Styles task pane and then display all the styles in alphabetical order. **Hint: Do this at the Style Pane Options dialog box.**

17. Select the second paragraph of text in the *FAIR COMPETITION* section and then apply the Block Text style. (If the Block Text style is not available, apply the Intense Quote style.)

18. Make sure the heading *Suppliers* displays on the same page as the paragraph of text that follows it.

19. Save the modified styles as a style set with the same name (your initials followed by *TRentals*). (At the Save as a New Style Set dialog box, click your style set name in the Content pane and then click the Save button. At the message asking if you want to replace the existing file, click the Yes button.)

20. Save, print, and then close **U-TRBusCode.docx**.

21. Press Ctrl + N to open a blank document and then delete the XXXTRentals style set (where your initials display in place of the *XXX*).

Create and Fill in a Purchase Order Form

1. Open **TTSPOForm.docx** and then save it as a template with the name **XXX-TTSTemplate** (with your initials in place of the *XXX*).
2. Create the form shown in Figure WB-U.2 with the following specifications:
   a. Insert a picture content control, date picker content control, and plain text content controls in the appropriate cells.
   b. Insert a drop-down list content control for *Company Status* with the choices *Bronze*, *Silver*, and *Gold*.
   c. Set the company name, *Terra Travel Services*, in 28 point Britannic Bold.
3. Protect the template.
4. Save and then close the template.
5. Create a form in a document from **XXX-TTSTemplate.dotx** with the following information:

Company Name	Banner Office Supplies
Date	(Insert the current date)
Company Status	(Choose the *Gold* option)
Description	6' x 4' dry eraser board
Quantity	1
Cost	$104.50
Description	Dry eraser markers, 12 pack
Quantity	3
Cost	$40.50
Description	Heavyweight file folders, 20 packs
Quantity	4
Cost	$51.96

6. Save the document and name it **U-TTSOrder**.
7. Print and then close **U-TTSOrder.docx**.

Figure WB-U.2 Assessment 6

Create and Fill in an Insurance Application Form

1. Open **LAProfApp.docx** and then save it as a template and name it **XXX-LAProfAppTemplate** (with your initials in place of the *XXX*).
2. Insert form fields in the template as shown in Figure WB-U.3 with the following specifications:
   a. Insert a text form field for *Client Number:* that specifies a maximum length of six characters.
   b. Insert a text form field for *Type of Deduction:* that specifies *Flat* as the default text.
   c. Insert a drop-down list form field for *Deduction Amount:* that includes the choices *None, $1,000, $2,500,* and *$5,000.*
   d. Insert four check boxes in the cell in the middle of the form table, as shown in Figure WB-U.3. **Hint: You can move the insertion point to a tab within a cell by pressing Ctrl + Tab.** Insert a check box form field in the cell immediately left of *AANA* that is checked by default.
   e. Insert the remaining text and check box form fields as shown in Figure WB-U.3.
3. Protect the template.
4. Save and then close **XXX-LAProfAppTemplate.dotx**.
5. Create a form document from **XXX-LAProfAppTemplate.dotx** and then insert the following information in the specified form fields:

First Name	Rachel
Middle Name	Brianne
Last Name	Hayward
Address	12091 South 234th Street, Fairbanks, AK 99704
Date of Birth	01/18/1982
Client Number	10-541
Current Date	(Insert the current date.)
Type of Deduction	(Leave *Flat* as the entry.)
Deduction Amount	(Choose *$5,000* at the drop-down list.)

   (Leave the check mark in the AANA check box and also insert a check mark in the APTA-PPS check box.)
   (Insert a check mark in the Occupational Therapist check box.)
6. Save the document with the name **U-LAProfAppHayward**.
7. Print and then close **U-LAProfAppHayward.docx**.

LIFETIME ANNUITY COMPANY
3310 CUSHMAN STREET ✧ FAIRBANKS, AK 99705 ✧ 907-555-8875

APPLICATION FOR PROFESSIONAL LIABILITY

First Name:	Middle Name:	Last Name:

Address:

Date of Birth:	Client Number:	Current Date:

Type of Deduction: Flat	Deduction Amount: None

Check if this insurance is to be part of a program.

☒ AANA   ☐ AAOMS   ☐ APTA-PPS   ☐ None

☐ Chiropractor	☐ Medical Technician
☐ Dental Assistant	☐ Nurse
☐ Dental Hygienist	☐ Nurse Practitioner
☐ Dietitian/Nutritionist	☐ Occupational Therapist
☐ Laboratory Director	☐ Optometrist
☐ Medical Office Assistant	☐ Paramedic/EMT

APPLICANT'S SIGNATURE: _____   DATE: _____

Assessment 8

Data Files

Create a Master Document and Subdocuments

1. Open **Resumes.docx** and then save it with the name **U-Resumes**.
2. Change to Outline view.
3. Assign Level 2 to the following headings:
   Preparing a Resume
   Nine Strategies for an Effective Resume
   Writing Style
   Writing Your Resume
4. Click the Show Document button in the Master Document group on the Outlining tab.

5. Create subdocuments by selecting the level 2 headings (and the body text and level 3 headings) and then clicking the Create button in the Master Document group.
6. Save and then close **U-Resumes.docx**.
7. Open **U-Resumes.docx** and then edit a subdocument by completing the following steps:
   a. Open the subdocument *Writing Your Resume.docx*.
   b. Delete the first paragraph below the *Name* subheading.
   c. Save, print, and then close the subdocument.
8. Display the document in Outline view, delete the subdocument *Preparing a Resume.docx*, and then close Outline view.
9. Save the document, print it without expanding the subdocuments, and then close **U-Resumes.docx**.

Writing Activities

Use Mail Merge to Create Letters to Volunteers

You are a volunteer coordinator for the Kentwood School District, and you have been asked to write a letter to the new reading volunteers listed in Figure WB-U.4, thanking them for their interest in volunteering for the reading literacy program and inviting them to an orientation meeting. Open a blank document, click the No Spacing style, and then save the document with the name **U-KSD-MD**. Create a data source file with the names, addresses, and grades shown in Figure WB-U.4.

In the main document letter, explain that during the orientation, volunteers will learn more about the reading program, including the program goals, the students served by the program, the reading levels included in the program, the time commitment required of volunteers, and the materials needed for the program. Include an If...Then...Else... field in the main document that inserts text stating that the orientation is Thursday, September 20, 2018, from 6:30 to 8:00 p.m. for volunteers interested in the K-3 grades or text stating that the orientation is Thursday, September 27, 2018, from 7:00 to 8:30 p.m.

Figure WB-U.4 Writing Activity 1

Ms. Karen Lyons
9023 South 42nd Street
Kentwood, MI 48933
Grades: K-3

Mr. Bryan Hamilton
11023 12th Avenue Northeast
Kentwood, MI 48920
Grades: 4-6

Mr. Richard Ulrich
453 Silverdale Road
Kentwood, MI 48930
Grades: 4-6

Mrs. Lindsay Childers
8931 133rd Place East
Kentwood, MI 48933
Grades: K-3

Mr. Juan Nunez
8329 Branchwood Drive
Kentwood, MI 48933
Grades: K-3

Ms. Lisa Taua
1129 Military Road South
Kentwood, MI 48930
Grades: K-3

Save the completed main document and then merge the main document with the data source file. Save the merged document and name it **U-KSDVolLtrs**. Print and then close **U-KSDVolLtrs.docx** and then save and close **U-KSD-MD.docx**.

Create a Contact Information Form

You work for the Evergreen Regional Center and are responsible for creating fill-in forms for the Records Department. Your supervisor has asked you to create a template for a fill-in form. Use **ERCFunding.docx** as a reference (for the image, font, and colors) and create a form that includes the following specifications:

- Use the information in the first cell in **ERCFunding.docx** for the first cell in the template you design.
- Add the title *Contact Information* to the form.
- Include the following fields:

    Name
    Birth date
    Marital status
    Gender
    Address
    Phone
    Email address
    Occupation
    Emergency contact
    Emergency phone

Save the completed form as a template and name it **U-ERCContactTemplate**. Open a document based on the template and then fill in the form. You determine the information to enter in the form. Save the completed form document and name it **U-ERCContactInfo**. Print and then close **U-ERCContactInfo.docx**.

Internet Research

Prepare a Donations Form

You work for Phoenix Rising and want to create a donation form template for the organization. Display images of donation forms on the Internet by going to www.google.com and then typing the search words *free donation form template*. At the list of sites that displays, click the <u>Images for free donation form template</u>. (If this hyperlink is not available, click a hyperlink that will display images of donation forms.) Look at the images that display and determine what information you want to include in your donation form. Open **PRLtrhd.docx** and then save it as a template with the name **U-PRDonationForm**.

Create a donation form in **U-PRDonationForm.dotx** that contains the information you determined was necessary for the form. Protect, save, and then close **U-PRDonationForm.dotx**. Open a document based on **U-PRDonationForm.dotx** and then save it with the name **U-PRForm**. Fill in the form with information of your choosing. Save, print, and then close **U-PRForm.docx**.

Job Study

Data Files

Develop and Format Company Documents

The Human Resources Manager is developing a policies and procedures manual for Phoenix Rising and you are responsible for formatting a document containing the beginning sections of the manual. Open **PRManual.docx** and then save it with the name **U-PRManual**.

- Phoenix Rising is misspelled throughout the document. Use a wildcard character to complete one find and replace that finds the following occurrences—*Pheonix Rising, Phoenix-Rising,* and *Phoenix Rasing*—and replaces them with *Phoenix Rising*.
- Create styles and/or record macros for formatting the manual that includes formatting the titles, headings, and subheadings. Apply the styles or macros to the appropriate text in the document.
- Run the accessibility checker on the document and correct any issues identified as errors or warnings *except* the warning that objects are not inline.

Save **U-PRManual.docx**. Print and then close the document.

One of your job responsibilities is to send a thank you letter to donors. Open **PRLtrhd.docx** and then save it with the name **U-PRDonorLtrMD**. Select **PRClientDonationTable.docx** as the data source file and insert appropriate fields in the main document to insert the address and greeting line.

Consider using information from the first two paragraph of text in the body of the letter in **PRLtrMD.docx**. Include another paragraph that thanks the donor for his or her contribution and includes the donation amount (the *Donation* field in the data source file). Insert an If…Then…Else field that inserts a sentence for any donations over $999 telling the donor that, with their generous donation, they are considered a platinum-level donor and their name will be added to the donation plaque that displays in Phoenix Rising's lobby. Use information in the third paragraph in **PRLtrMD.docx** to close the letter and include the same complimentary close (with the name *Neela Shame* and her title, *Executive Director*). Include your reference initials at the end of the document. Merge the main document with the data source file and then save the merged letters as **U-PRThankYouLtrs**. Print and then close **U-PRThankYouLtrs.docx** and then save and close **U-PRDonorLtrMD.docx**.